Ghost
Bat in a
Gum
Tree

by Benette W. Tiffault

illustrated by Peter Grosshauser

FALCON

HELENA, MONTANA

In the **first** hour of Earth Day, my true love saved for me

a ghost bat

in

a

gum tree.

In the **second**

hour of Earth Day,

my true love

saved for me

two

bandicoots,

and a ghost bat in a gum tree.

squeak

In the **third** hour of Earth Day, my true love saved for me

three manatees,

two bandicoots,

and a ghost bat in a gum tree.

In the **fourth** hour of Earth Day,
my true love saved for me

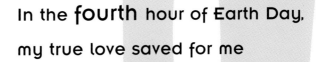

four panda bears,

three manatees,

two bandicoots,

and a ghost bat
in a gum tree.

In the **fifth** hour
of Earth Day,
my true love
saved for me

five
golden
marmosets,

four panda bears,

three manatees,

two bandicoots,

and

a ghost bat
in a gum tree.

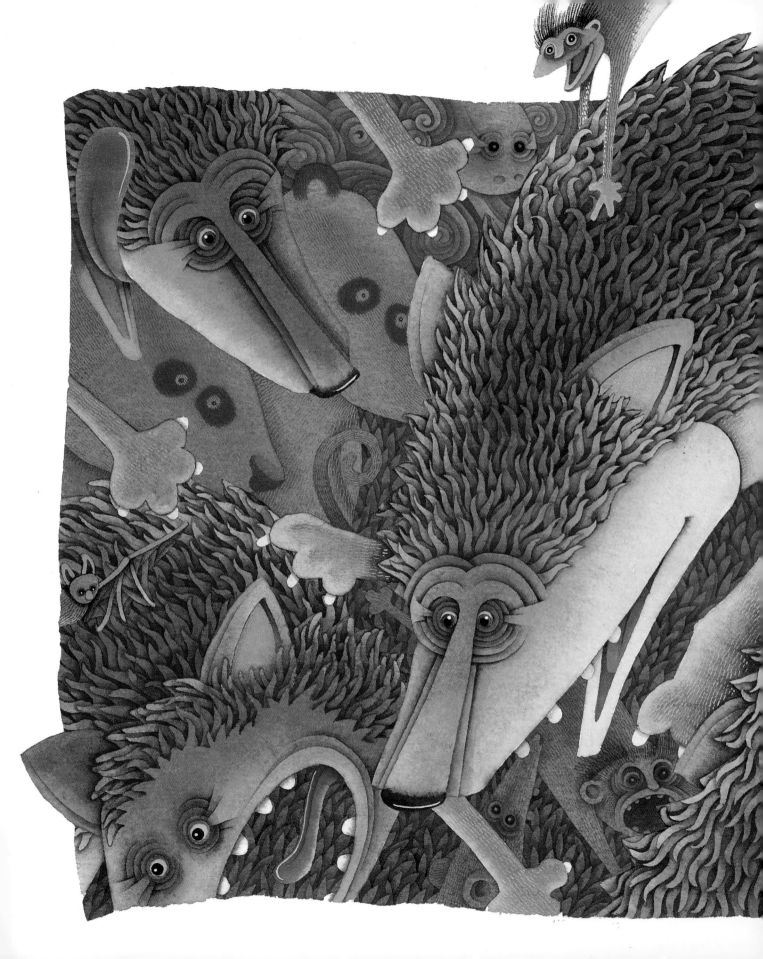

In the **sixth** hour
of Earth Day,
my true love
saved for me

six
wolves
a-playing,

five golden marmosets,

four panda bears,

three manatees,

two bandicoots,

and a
ghost bat
in a gum tree.

In the **seventh** hour of Earth Day, my true love saved for me

seven sloths a-slinking,

six wolves a-playing,

five golden marmosets,

four panda bears,

three manatees,

two bandicoots,

and a
ghost bat
in a gum tree.

In the **eighth** hour of Earth Day,
my true love saved for me

eight
parrots
preening,

seven sloths a-slinking,

six wolves a-playing,

five golden marmosets,

four panda bears,

three manatees,

two bandicoots,

and a
ghost bat
in a gum tree.

AWK!

In the **ninth** hour
of Earth Day,
my true love
saved for me

nine humpbacks puffing,

eight parrots preening,

seven sloths a-slinking,

six wolves a-playing,

five golden marmosets,

four panda bears,

three manatees,

two bandicoots,

and a
ghost bat
in a gum tree.

In the **tenth** hour
of Earth Day,
my true love
saved for me

ten chimps a-chomping,

nine humpbacks puffing,

eight parrots preening,

seven sloths a-slinking,

six wolves a-playing,

five golden marmosets,

four panda bears,

three manatees,

two bandicoots,

and a ghost bat
in a
gum tree.

In the **eleventh** hour
of Earth Day, my true love
saved for me

eleven
lemurs
leaping,

ten chimps a-chomping,

nine humpbacks puffing,

eight parrots preening,

seven sloths a-slinking,

six wolves a-playing,

five golden marmosets,

four panda bears,

three manatees,

two bandicoots,

and a ghost bat
in a gum tree.

In the **twelfth** hour
of Earth Day, my true love
saved for me

twelve rhinos roaming,

eleven lemurs leaping,

ten chimps a-chomping,

nine humpbacks puffing,

eight parrots preening,

seven sloths a-slinking,

six wolves a-playing,

five golden marmosets,

four panda bears,

three manatees,

two bandicoots,

and a
ghost bat
in a
gum
tree.

Threatened, Endangered, *or* Extinct?

A **species** is a group of related animals or plants that reproduces itself. If a species' population starts to decrease, the species is labeled **threatened**. If the species' numbers become very small, it is called **endangered**. An **endangered species** may soon become **extinct**, with none of its members left anywhere on earth.

How does a species become extinct?

Every species lives in a balanced community of plants and animals known as a **habitat**. When a habitat is changed or destroyed, it becomes difficult, and often impossible, for species that live there to survive.

Loss of habitat is the most common cause of extinction. When places such as the rain forest are destroyed so people can sell its trees or develop its land, many species, including some we never knew existed, are lost forever.

Other dangerous threats to species' futures are poachers—hunters who steal or illegally kill animals to make money. Car and jet emissions, toxic chemicals from factories, and pesticides also pose problems to our Earth's plants and animals.

Scientists estimate that 1 species becomes extinct every hour of the day, and if nothing is done, up to half the Earth's species may be extinct within 10 years.

Species
Specifics

Ghost Bat (Endangered)

Ghost bats are the only meat-eating bats in Australia, where they live, feed, and raise their young in caves or abandoned mine shafts. Using its 2-foot wing span, the ghost bat swoops around in search of its favorite foods: large insects, lizards, frogs, birds, and small mammals. Limestone miners are disturbing ghost bats' roosts, threatening the species' survival.

Gum Tree (Eucalyptus) (Threatened)

Rot-fungus disease threatens the once common gum tree, known more formally as the eucalyptus. Native to Australia, the gum tree can grow as tall as a 25-story building (300 feet). The gum tree's wood, similar to mahogany, is used to make ships, telegraph poles, railroad ties, piers, and fences. The oil from its leaves is used in cough drops and fragrances. Some hopeful news for the gum tree: it has been successfully transplanted in tropic and sub-tropic environments.

Bandicoot (Endangered)

The bandicoot (known to Australians as the bilby) is a marsupial, making it cousin to the kangaroo. Bandicoots forage at night, using their long, pointy snouts to find tasty plants and insects. European settlers in Australia brought with them foxes and rabbits, which preyed upon the bandicoots and took over their burrows. To make matters worse, farmers who considered bandicoots pests also destroyed them. Loss of habitat because of human development has also made bandicoots nearly extinct.

Manatee (Endangered)

Nicknamed the "sea cow," the beloved manatee is known for its gentle nature and enormous size. Even though manatees have been legally protected for more than 100 years, they may possibly become extinct before long. Loss of food supply due to pollution and development is the biggest risk to the manatees' future. Found in coastal shallows and river estuaries, when manatees float to the surface to take a breath, they are often seriously harmed or killed by speedboats.

Panda (Endangered)

Few giant pandas remain in the bamboo forests of southeast China. Bamboo is the panda's favorite food, and a full-grown, 400-pound panda eats about 40 pounds a day. As bamboo is cut down for fuel and to make space for farmland in China, pandas are disappearing. Poachers who shoot pandas and sell their fur also put this species in serious danger. Zoos are trying to help the species survive and reproduce, but pandas rarely give birth in captivity.

Golden Marmoset (Threatened)

Native to the tropical rain forests of South America, the golden marmoset is one of the world's smallest and most unusual monkeys, weighing less than 1 pound and sporting a 16-inch tail on its 12-inch body. The golden marmoset's diet consists of fruit, insects, and spiders. Male marmosets help out during their youngsters' births, and they carry newborns on their backs. Rain forest destruction has decreased the number of golden marmosets, threatening their existence.

Wolf (Endangered)

Wolf packs, like families, include a father, mother, young wolves, pups, aunts, and uncles. Each wolf knows and respects its place in the pack. Only the alpha wolf leader and his mate have pups, then others in the pack help care for them. Development and pollution have destroyed much of the wolves' habitat in the contiguous United States, where they have also been hunted, trapped, and poisoned. Despite people's fear of these predators, there is no recorded instance of a wolf killing a human.

Sloth (Endangered)

Found mainly in Central and South American rain forests, sloths are nocturnal mammals that like to hang upside down in trees. When they move, they do it very slowly. The sloths' diet of twigs, leaves, and fruit takes more than a month for them to digest. Their fur is covered with green algae, a natural camouflage in the forest. Rain forest destruction, causing loss of habitat, has put the sloth's future in peril.

Parrot (Endangered)

Parrots, famous for mimicking human voices and other sounds, mate for life, usually 70 to 100 years. Found in tropical climates around the world, many species of parrots are in immediate danger of extinction, and most of the rest are threatened because of habitat loss. Developers are cutting down the parrots' rain forest homes for lumber and farmland. Parrots are also disappearing because they're popular pets, often sold by poachers for thousands of dollars.

Humpback Whale (Endangered)

Humpback whales live in the Atlantic and Pacific oceans, and in the fall and winter, they migrate to the tropics where they mate and raise their calves. Males are known for their moaning, melodic songs, which they use to communicate with each other. In place of teeth, humpbacks have an unusual bone structure that they use to strain their tiny food, called plankton, from the water. Whalers have hunted humpbacks to near extinction for their bones, meat, and blubber.

Chimp (Endangered)

Chimpanzees, one of Africa's great apes, live both in trees and on the ground, usually in groups of 4 or 5. The playful chimp is also resourceful, using crumpled leaves for sponges and shady branches for umbrellas. Mothers teach their young how to use tools such as stone or wood hammers to crack open fruits and nuts, their usual diet. Without a major effort to preserve the rain forest, the chimp faces extinction.

Lemur (Endangered)

A relative of apes and monkeys, the lemur lives on the island of Madagascar, off the southeastern coast of Africa. It is the only mammal in the world that acts like a woodpecker when looking for food, tapping its long fingers on tree trunks to roust tasty insects. Madagascar's human population is growing very rapidly. The beautiful rain forests, no longer rich with bamboo, are being chopped down for wood, fuel, and development, which seriously endangers the lemur.

Rhinoceros (Endangered)

The average rhinoceros can run 30 miles per hour, even though it weighs close to 5 tons. Rhinos have poor eyesight, but they have keen senses of smell and hearing. The rhino's horn, its trademark feature, is made of tightly-packed hair. Sadly, poachers kill rhinos to steal their horns, which often sell for more money than gold. More than 100 species of rhinos once roamed the earth, but today only 5 species remain: 3 in Asia and 2 in Africa.

How can you help?

Write to the groups below to learn how you can help save threatened and endangered species:

DEFENDERS OF WILDLIFE
1244 19th Street, NW
Washington, D.C. 20036

GREENPEACE
1436 U Street, NW
Washington, D.C. 20009

NATIONAL WILDLIFE FEDERATION
1400 16th Street, NW
Washington, D.C. 20036

THE NATURE CONSERVANCY
1800 North Kent Street
Arlington, Virginia 22209

RAIN FOREST ACTION NETWORK
466 Green Street
San Francisco, California 94133

SIERRA CLUB
730 Polk Street
San Francisco, California 94109

WHALE ADOPTION PROJECT
INTERNATIONAL WILDLIFE COALITION
P.O. Box 388
634 North Falmouth Highway
North Falmouth, Massachusetts 02556

WORLD WILDLIFE FUND
1250 24th Street, NW
Washington, D.C. 20037

About the Author

Benette W. Tiffault teaches writing at the State University of New York College of Environmental Science & Forestry and Syracuse University. This is Benette's sixth children's book, and she wrote it during a family road trip with the help of her kids, Eli and Kallie. For fun, she enjoys listening to her husband Lee's bands, hiking in the forest, and daydreaming, which she claims is an essential activity of writers. She loves being a children's author, mostly because it means she can stay a kid forever and nobody will mind.

photo by Russ McConnell

About the Illustrator

This is Peter Grosshauser's second children's book. He has illustrated many articles for children's magazines and is the creator of the "Wild Willie" comic strip in *W.O.W.* magazine. He lives in Montana with his wife and their two dogs, two cats, and bird. In his spare time, Peter enjoys picking all the fur and feathers out of his paints and brushes.